Read & Resp

Ages
5–7

Read & Respond

Ages
5–7

Author: Sarah Snashall and Huw Thomas

Commissioning Editor: Rachel Mackinnon

Development Editor: Marion Archer

Editor: Sarah Sodhi

Series Designer: Anna Oliwa

Designer: Anna Oliwa

Illustrations: Mike Phillips (Beehive Illustration)

Text © 2012, Sarah Snashall and Huw Thomas © 2012, Scholastic Ltd

Designed using Adobe InDesign

Published by Scholastic Ltd,
Book End, Range Road, Witney,
Oxfordshire OX29 0YD
www.scholastic.co.uk

Printed by Bell & Bain
1 2 3 4 5 6 7 8 9   2 3 4 5 6 7 8 9 0 1

British Library Cataloguing-in-Publication Data
A catalogue record for this book is available from
the British Library.
ISBN 978-1407-12729-3

Acknowledgements
The publishers gratefully acknowledge permission to reproduce the following copyright material: **Penguin Books** for the use of the cover, text extracts and illustrations from *Each Peach Pear Plum* by Janet and Allan Ahlberg. Text and illustrations © 1978, Janet and Allan Ahlberg (1978, Viking Kestrel). Every effort has been made to trace copyright holders for the works reproduced in this book, and the publishers apologise for any inadvertent omissions.

Each Peach Pear Plum

About the book

Each Peach Pear Plum is peopled with favourite fairy characters. The reader's existing knowledge of the characters and the detailed illustrations allow the children, even those with emergent literacy skills, to discuss character and how it relates to plot. The illustrations are filled with humorous details. They cleverly and perfectly illustrate the text, while also telling their own story. The illustrations provide excellent opportunities for early readers to investigate plot. Children may also like Allan Ahlberg's *Ten in a Bed* (illustrated by Andre Amstutz), which is also peopled with story characters.

Like other favourite Janet and Allan Ahlberg books (for example, *Peepo* and *The Jolly Postman*), *Each Peach Pear Plum* is part-story and part-game. The reader has to actively take part in the book – most simply by playing a game of 'I spy', but also by working out the story that is told through the illustrations rather than the text.

Within the illustrations, Tom Thumb eats jam at Mother Hubbard's house, while she is in the cellar and Cinderella is cleaning the stairs. Through the window of Mother Hubbard's house we see the Three Bears go out hunting. Baby Bear accidently sets off his gun and shoots down Baby Bunting's crib that falls into the river. As the bears continue their walk, we see Bo-Peep, Jack and Jill and Robin Hood, who is trying to shoot down the Wicked Witch. On their way back, the Three Bears rescue Baby Bunting from the river and everyone meets at Mother Hubbard's for Plum Pie.

About the author and illustrator

Husband and wife team, Allan Ahlberg (born 1938) and Janet Ahlberg (1944–1994) worked together creating children's books for 20 years. Allan Ahlberg was born in Croydon and grew up in the Midlands. Janet (born Janet Hall) was born in Leicester and grew up there. Janet and Allan met at teacher training college.

Allan wrote the books and Janet illustrated them. Allan said that it took him one day to write the text for *Each Peach Pear Plum* and it took Janet six months to illustrate it, but they split the money fifty-fifty! Janet won the Kate Greenaway Medal in 1978 for her artwork.

They began working together when Janet asked Allan to write something for her to illustrate, and continued their partnership until Janet's premature death. After many rejection letters, their first three manuscripts were accepted in the same week: *The Old Joke Book* (Penguin); *The Vanishment of Thomas Tull* (A&C Black) and *Burglar Bill* (Heinemann).

Together they wrote 37 books, including many bestsellers. *The Jolly Postman*, a book of letters and cards inspired by their daughter's fascination with letters, has sold more than six million copies. Since Janet's death, Allan has worked with a number of other illustrators.

Facts and figures
Title: *Each Peach Pear Plum*.
Author: Allan Ahlberg.
Illustrator: Janet Ahlberg.
First published: 1978.
Awards: Kate Greenaway Award in 1978.

Guided reading

Before reading

Show the book to the children. How many of them are familiar with it? If any children know it already, discuss how they know it and where they know if from (for instance, from the library, home or a relative's house).

First reading

Read the opening rhyme and find Tom Thumb. Read the next page and find Mother Hubbard. Carry on reading, stopping near the middle to ask: *What is the pattern of the book?* (Each page shows the character who was hiding on the previous page and tells the reader who's hiding now.) Read to the end of the book, finding the characters on each page as you go.

Establish that this is a poem. Talk about the rhymes in the book. Go through the book, page by page, and ask the children to pick out the rhyming pairs (such as *cellar/Cinderella, stairs/Bears, wood/Hood*). Go around the group and together try to come up with a rhyme for everyone's name.

Second reading

Each Peach Pear Plum is told as much through its illustrations as it is through the text. In a second reading of *Each Peach Pear Plum*, take the time to explore the detail in the illustrations and talk about who the characters are and how their behaviour is linked to their nursery rhyme or story.

Look first at the cover and enjoy the details together. Who can say where the various animals and items appear in the story? Can they talk about Mother Hubbard's dog, the Wicked Witch's cat, Bo-Peep's sheep, Robin Hood's horn and Father Bear's bag? Read the opening rhyme and find Tom Thumb again. Ask: *Who is Tom Thumb?* The Tom Thumb fairy tale is rather extended and complicated. Tom Thumb, a boy no bigger than his mother's thumb, loves adventures, but gets more than he bargained for when he is stolen

by birds, swallowed by a cow and fights other animals. Alternatively, the children might like to think of him as Tommy Thumb. (Tommy Thumb, Tommy Thumb, Where are you? Here I am! Here I am! How do you do?) Ask: *What sort of tree is Tom Thumb in?* (A peach tree.) Pick out and identify the types of fruit tree in the orchard: peach, pear and plum. Ask: *What other details can you see in the picture? What are the rabbits doing? What's Tom doing? Who's left the ladder against the plum tree? How's Tom going to get down? Who picked the basket of plums?*

Turn to the next page. Spot Mother Hubbard again. Remember the appropriate rhyme:

Old Mother Hubbard
Went to the cupboard
To get the poor dog a bone
But when she came there
The cupboard was bare
So the poor little dog had none.

Ask: *Does this picture fit with the rhyme?* (No, things seem to be looking up for Mother Hubbard.) *What is in the cupboard?* (Dog food.) *What can you spot by the door?* (The plums Tom Thumb picked on the previous page.) *What do you think Mother Hubbard might be cooking?* (Plum Pie.) *Look out the door of Mother Hubbard's cottage – what can you see?* (The orchard.) Can the children find the orchard and Mother Hubbard's cottage in the picture on the title page?

Turn the page and read the next rhyme. Once they've found Cinderella, discuss with the children why Cinderella might be cleaning, linking it to the story that they know about her. Quickly recap on the story. Look again at the detail of the picture. Ask: *What does Mother Hubbard have in her cellar?*

On the next page, can anyone say why there are three bowls above the text? Ask: *Who knows the story of 'Goldilocks and the Three Bears'?* Make the link that the bears are out for a walk. Turn the page to look at where they go on their walk. Ask: *What story is happening here that only takes place in the pictures and not the text?*

Guided reading

(Baby Bear has tripped over a log and set off his gun, bringing down Baby Bunting's basket.) Remind the children of the nursery rhyme 'Bye, Baby Bunting':

Bye, Baby Bunting,
Daddy's gone a-hunting,
Gone to get a rabbit skin
To wrap the Baby Bunting in.

Read the next four pages, pointing out how the small images on the left-hand pages are always linked to the characters who are hiding on the right. Can the children say what Bo-Peep is doing in the field, and then while sitting on the well? (Looking for her sheep.) Recite the nursery rhyme together:

Little Bo-Peep has lost her sheep
And doesn't know where to find them;
Leave them alone, and they'll come home,
Wagging their tails behind them.

Ask: *What are Jack and Jill doing when we first see them?* (Falling down the hill.) Point out to the children that the characters are all doing what they should be according to their nursery rhyme or story. Sing together the nursery rhyme 'Jack and Jill':

Jack and Jill went up the hill
To fetch a pail of water.
Jack fell down and broke his crown
And Jill came tumbling after.

Turn to the picture of Jack and Jill in the ditch. Point out the fact that Jack is holding his head – remember together that Jack hurts his 'crown'. Look at the expression on the Wicked Witch's face. Ask: *What might she be thinking?* In the next picture, why do they think that Robin Hood is trying to shoot down the Wicked Witch? Ask: *What is the Wicked Witch thinking now?*

Pause on the picture of Robin Hood's den to enjoy the details: the picture on the tree, the vase on the shelf, his comfy cushion, the scared rabbits and Baby Bear still falling over and shooting in random directions in the background.

Read to the end of the book, pointing out the happy story of Baby Bunting being rescued (the only thing the Three Bears catch on their hunting trip). Name all the characters eating the Plum Pie and enjoy the rabbits finishing off the pie on the last page.

Character meeting character

Challenge the children to remember the characters in the book. Can they remember everyone? (Tom Thumb, Mother Hubbard, Cinderella, the Three Bears, Baby Bunting, Bo-Peep, Jack and Jill, the Wicked Witch and Robin Hood.) Can anyone succeed in naming all the characters in one go?

Remind the children that the real story of *Each Peach Pear Plum* takes place in the illustrations rather than the text. Can the children think of other stories where the illustration tells a different or more complicated story than the text? (Possibly *Once Upon a Time* by John Prater or *Suddenly* by Colin McNaughton.)

Apart from Baby Bunting being knocked down and then rescued by the Three Bears, in what other ways do the various characters connect? Ask: *Who meets whom? Do the characters know each other?* Encourage the children to ask or answer questions about the characters. For example, ask: *Why do the Three Bears look in Mother Hubbard's window? Does Cinderella see them? Do Jack and Jill see the Wicked Witch?*

Continuing to focus on the characters in the book, play a game of 'Find me…'. In pairs, ask the children to challenge their partner to find someone in the book who is doing something. Each request is phrased as a clue. For example, 'Find me someone who looks after animals', or 'Find me someone who can fly'.

Ask the children to follow the day of one of the characters, such as the Three Bears or Robin Hood. Ask: *What did they see? What did they do? How did their day end?*

Guided reading

The animals

Stories in this book also take place within the animal kingdom. Look together at where the bluebirds fly. Ask: *Where are the rabbits in this book? Who are they frightened of and why? What does the frog find?* (Baby Bunting's dummy.) *Last time we saw the dummy it was safe in Baby Bunting's cot – how did the frog end up with it?*

Finally

Invite the children to vote on a favourite page from the picture book and to explain the reasoning for their selection. Ask: *What do you like best about the book?* Perhaps the children enjoy the way the text rhymes, the 'I spy' game, or the story told through the illustrations?

Shared reading

Extract 1

- Display Extract 1 and establish where this text comes from. (The back cover.)
- Ask: *In what way is this back cover blurb unusual?* Elicit that it is a poem. Pick out the rhyming words together and ask for volunteers to circle them. Discuss the pattern of the rhyme. (Alternate lines.)
- Discuss how the game 'I spy' works. Does everyone agree on the rules or do the children have any variations? Play a quick game of 'I spy'.

- Ask the children to pretend that they don't know the book. What sort of book might they expect from this blurb? Ask: *How can you play 'I spy' with a book? What other books do you know where you have to find things in the pictures?*
- Invite them to create a simple four-line rhyme for the book following a similar pattern ('Who will you find/Within this book?/Who has got/A shepherd's crook?'; 'Which old friends/Are trying to hide?/You will soon/Find out inside.')

Extract 2

- Invite the children to share some of the rhymes that they know, such as playground rhymes, clapping games or skipping rhymes. Choose various children to tell the class about the ones they are familiar with.
- Display Extract 2 and establish that these are the opening lines of the book.
- Talk again about the 'I spy' game that you played in the last session (with Extract 1) and remember that this book is based on that game.
- Recall the way characters are hidden in the book. Who can remember the name of

one character? Who is hidden in this picture? Establish the type of tree that Tom Thumb is in. (A peach tree.) What are the other trees? (Pear trees and plum trees.) Make the link with the title of the book.
- Circle the rhyme and discuss the two spellings of the sound 'um'. Can the children suggest any other words ending in 'um'? (For example, 'drum', 'hum', 'come', 'gum', 'dumb', 'slum', 'glum'.) Sort the words out into the different spellings of 'um' and discuss the different spellings of the same sound.

Extract 3

- Re-read *Each Peach Pear Plum* and then display an enlarged version of Extract 3, covering up or folding over the right-hand text.
- Read the left-hand text to the class and ask: *What do we know about the illustration from reading this text? Who is in the picture?* (Cinderella.)
- Ask: *Who will be on the next double-page? How do we know this?* (The Three Bears. We know that the character hiding in one picture becomes the main character for the next.) *Will Cinderella be in the next picture?* (No, as Cinderella has previously hidden and been revealed.)
- Reveal the text on the right-hand side and have a similar discussion with the children. Ask: *What*

can we work out about the next double-page? How will it be linked to the right-hand extract? (It will involve Baby Bunting.)
- Talk about the characters named here. Ask: *What do we know about them from elsewhere?* Recite the nursery rhyme 'Bye, Baby Bunting'. (See page 5.)
- Organise the children into a circle. Start a game in which you say something about the child next to you and then mention the next child along. For example, 'Josh likes football and next to him is Jai'. Encourage the next child (Josh) to say something like, 'Jai's got a rabbit and next to him is Dionne'. Create a circle rhyme in this way.

Extract 1

In this book
With your little eye
Take a look
And play 'I spy'

ISBN 978-0-140-50919-9

9 780140 509199

U.K. £5.99   CAN. $7.99

Text and illustration © 1978, Janet and Allan Ahlberg.

SCHOLASTIC
www.scholastic.co.uk

Extract 2

Each Peach Pear Plum
I spy Tom Thumb

Text and illustration © 1978, Janet and Allan Ahlberg.

Extract 3

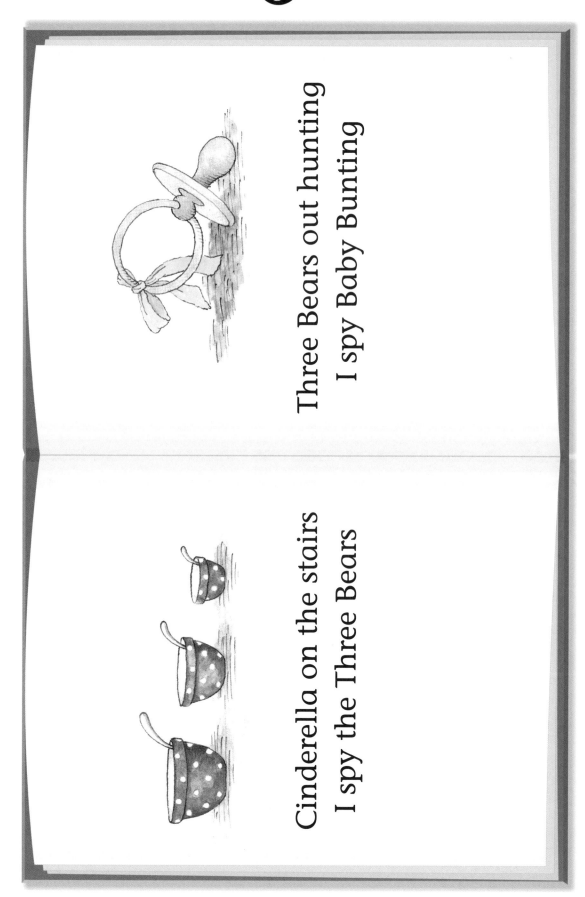

Three Bears out hunting
I spy Baby Bunting

Cinderella on the stairs
I spy the Three Bears

Text and illustrations © 1978, Janet and Allan Ahlberg.

SCHOLASTIC
www.scholastic.co.uk

Plot, character and setting

Plum Land

Objective: To identify the main events and characters in stories.
What you need: Copies of *Each Peach Pear Plum*, photocopiable page 28.
Cross-curricular link: Geography.

What to do
● Re-read *Each Peach Pear Plum*. Look together at the view of 'Plum Land' on the title page. Can anyone point out a place where something in the story happened?
● Ask the children to work in pairs and hand out copies of the book (or photocopiable page 28). Invite them to use the title page and identify what happens at the following locations: main cottage, well, bottom of the hill, by the woods and by the stone bridge.
● Next, challenge the children to highlight the path that the Three Bears took.
● Come back together as a group and confirm the locations by looking at the correct page in the book. Encourage the children to pick out small details and to talk about any other locations.
● Look at the second house shown on the title page. Ask: *Does anything happen in this house?* (No, it is not in the story.) Discuss who could live there and what might happen there in a sequel.
● Confirm the path that the Three Bears take and together discuss where Bo-Peep and the other characters went. (Past the cottage, looking in the window as they go, over the stone bridge, into the woods, and then back again over the bridge to the cottage.)

Differentiation
For older/more confident learners: Encourage the children to make links between the detail in individual illustrations and the view of 'Plum Land'. For example, can they see the two trees where Baby Bear trips? Where did Tom Thumb pick the plums?
For younger/less confident learners: Allow the children to concentrate on finding just two locations on the map that are involved in the story.

Pears before plums

Objective: To recognise the main elements that shape different texts.
What you need: Copies of *Each Peach Pear Plum*, photocopiable page 15.

What to do
● Invite the children to try to remember the order that events happen in the book.
● Hand out photocopiable page 15 to pairs of children and ask them to cut out the boxes and arrange the events into the order they take place in the story.
● Once they've agreed on an order, invite them to retell the story together.
● As a class, look at the different versions of the order the children may have. Read the story and retell the events verbally.
● If necessary, let the children re-order the events again.
● Discuss which events were easier to remember than others and why this might be. The events around the Three Bears, Robin Hood and Baby Bunting will probably have been easier as they form a continuous narrative.
● Some events might need to be discussed further. For example, does Baby Bear trip before or after Baby Bunting falls out of the tree?

Differentiation
For older/more confident learners: Invite the children to use their copies of the book to suggest other events that could be added to the timeline.
For younger/less confident learners: Let the children focus on working with the first four events.

Plot, character and setting

Left-hand pictures

> **Objective:** To explain organisational features of texts, including alphabetical order, layout, diagrams, captions, hyperlinks and bullet points.
> **What you need:** Copies of *Each Peach Pear Plum*, scissors, glue, paper and photocopiable page 16.

What to do

● As a class, look at the small motifs on each left-hand page. Discuss the connection between the motif and the characters on a couple of the pages.
● Hand out photocopiable page 16 to pairs of children and invite them to cut out the boxes and to match each motif with its character.
● Once the pairs have agreed, provide glue for them to stick their answers on a sheet of paper.
● When the children have finished, agree together which motif goes with which character. Discuss the children's reasoning. How often is the connection something that they knew previously from outside the book? Talk about how well they know the characters in the story.
● Look through the book together and check that the agreed answers are correct.

> **Differentiation**
> **For older/more confident learners:** Encourage the children to annotate each pair with a word or an image to explain the connection.
> **For younger/less confident learners:** Ask the children to focus on just four pairs.

Building words

> **Objective:** To explore how particular words are used, including words and expressions with similar meanings.
> **What you need:** Copies of *Each Peach Pear Plum*, scissors and photocopiable page 17.

What to do

● Verbally recall the rhyme of the book, or read it aloud to the class. Talk about the rhyming pattern of the book. First, a place is mentioned, then a new character is introduced who rhymes with that place (where the last character was found).
● Hand out photocopiable page 17 and ask the children to cut out the boxes. Explain that words from *Each Peach Pear Plum* have been split into their beginning and ending sounds (onset and rime).
● Invite the children to try different phonic combinations using the cut-out boxes to search for words they recall from the story.
● Remind them about the different sounds that 'c' can make (they are searching for 'cellar').
● Emphasise that they are looking only for words from *Each Peach Pear Plum*. For example, they will be able to make the word 'will', but 'will' is not used in the story. If they are trying to choose between two word options, such as 'will' and 'hill', suggest that they try to recall the names of the characters. If they think of 'Jill', can they now remember which word is used to rhyme with 'Jill' in the book?
● Discuss their answers as a class.

> **Differentiation**
> **For older/more confident learners:** Let the children try one rime at a time, making words using all the onsets until they find one that fits the story.
> **For younger/less confident learners:** Provide the children with a list of the character names and objects that they are looking to rhyme with: 'Cinderella', 'Three Bears', 'Baby Bunting', 'Jack and Jill', 'Wicked Witch', 'Robin Hood', 'again', 'Plum Pie' and 'everyone'.

Plot, character and setting

I spy Plum Pie

> **Objective:** To identify the main events and characters in stories, and find specific information in simple texts.
> **What you need:** Copies of *Each Peach Pear Plum* and photocopiable page 18.
> **Cross-curricular link:** Art.

What to do

● Explain to the children that they are going to play 'I spy' with *Each Peach Pear Plum*.
● Hand out photocopiable page 18 and explain that all of these items can be found within the illustrations in the book.
● Before trying to find the items, read the words together as a class to ensure that everyone knows what each item is.

● Discuss the activity with the group. Can anyone predict where some of these items will be located?
● Let the children work through their individual copies of *Each Peach Pear Plum*, ticking off the items as they find them.
● If appropriate, create an element of competition. For instance, who can find the first ten items the quickest?

> **Differentiation**
> **For older/more confident learners:** Encourage the children to predict where each item will be located in the book and open it up in (nearly) the right place.
> **For younger/less confident learners:** Reduce by half the number of items the children need to find.

Character traits

> **Objective:** To identify the main events and characters in stories, and find specific information in simple texts.
> **What you need:** Copies of *Each Peach Pear Plum*, photocopiable page 16, card, scissors and pens.
> **Cross-curricular link:** PSHE.

What to do

● Together, recall the characters that we meet in *Each Peach Pear Plum*.
● Ask for volunteers to describe what a couple of the characters are like. For example, 'Robin Hood is relaxed' and 'Baby Bunting is peaceful'.
● Create a set of nine character cards by re-using photocopiable page 16 (you will need to add cards for Baby Bunting and Tom Thumb).
● Ask the children to work in pairs and give each pair a set of character cards.
● Tell the children to write a one-word description on the back of each of the nine character cards.
● As a class, compare the various traits that have

been given to each character. Stick the words on large pieces of paper – one for each character. How many descriptions do you have that are the same? Are there any that contradict each other? Discuss this as a group.
● Next, create a set of cards with just a one-word description on. For example, they might include: 'clumsy', 'brave', 'worried', 'sticky', 'nosey', 'surprised' and 'delighted'.
● Give various children a different description card each and ask them to stick it on one of the character sheets. Does anyone disagree with their decision? Discuss their thinking as a group.

> **Differentiation**
> **For older/more confident learners:** Challenge the children to write two words for each character, for example 'Robin Hood is relaxed and happy'.
> **For younger/less confident learners:** Provide the children with fewer character cards, as appropriate. (Perhaps ranging from three to five cards.)

Plot, character and setting

In and over

> **Objective:** To use syntax and context when reading for meaning.
> **What you need:** Copies of *Each Peach Pear Plum*, blank cards and small object, such as a coin, and a container.

What to do
● Talk to the children about prepositions. Remind them that these are words we use to describe where something is positioned, such as 'over', 'at', 'under', and so on.
● Take a small object and a container and use these to demonstrate different positions. Together create a list of as many prepositions as possible.
● Ask the children to work in small groups and challenge them to see how many of the words on the list they can find in *Each Peach Pear Plum*.

● Provide the children with small blank cards and invite them to write the prepositions that they find on separate cards.
● Tell the groups to shuffle their cards and place them face down on the table. Invite the children to take turns to select a card and recall who or what was 'over', 'under', 'down', and so on. Let them check their answers in the book.

> **Differentiation**
> **For older/more confident learners:** Challenge the children to put the prepositions in the order that they occur in the story.
> **For younger/less confident learners:** Steer the children towards finding three prepositions in the book. You might like to provide them with three, such as 'in', 'on' and 'over'.

Asking why

> **Objective:** To give some reasons why things happen or characters change.
> **What you need:** Copies of *Each Peach Pear Plum* and sticky notes.

What to do
● Ask the children some 'why' questions about the book. For example: *Why did Baby Bunting's basket fall from the tree? Why is Tom Thumb in the cupboard? Why does the frog have a dummy? Why does Robin Hood shoot at the Witch? Why is the Witch in the bush?*
● Ask: *Which of these questions can we answer?* (Why Baby Bunting fell, and perhaps why the frog has a dummy.) *Which ones do we not know the answer to?* (All the others.)
● Invite the children to work in small groups of three or four and to come up with as many 'why' questions as they can about the book.

● Encourage them to choose their four best questions. Remind them that the answer to the question does not need to be in the book.
● Come together as a class and ask each group to ask their questions.
● Write the questions on sticky notes and stick them in a class copy of *Each Peach Pear Plum*. Create additional questions so that each double-page spread has at least one question on it.
● Provide time for the children to think up answers to as many of the questions as possible.

> **Differentiation**
> **For older/more confident learners:** Ask the children to rank their own questions in order of most- to least-interesting.
> **For younger/less confident learners:** Allow the children to concentrate on composing one or two good questions.

SECTION
4

Pears before plums

● Cut out the event boxes and place them in the correct order.

Baby Bear tripped over a log.	Jack and Jill fell down the hill.
Baby Bunting fell from a tree.	Robin Hood read a book.
Baby Bunting floated down river.	Robin Hood shot an arrow at the Wicked Witch.
The Bears took Baby Bunting out of the river.	The Three Bears looked through a window.
Everyone ate Plum Pie.	Tom Thumb ate jam in the cupboard.

Plot, character and setting

Left-hand pictures

● Cut out the boxes below. Match the pictures to their correct characters.

Three Bears	
Robin Hood	
Cinderella	
Wicked Witch	
Bo-Peep	
Jack and Jill	
Mother Hubbard	

Illustrations © 2012, Mike Phillips (Beehive Illustration).

Building words

- Cut out the boxes below. Match the beginning and ending sounds to find words from *Each Peach Pear Plum.*

Beginning sound			Ending sound		
c	st	h	ill	en	un
h	d	w	ellar	y	airs
d	dr	s	ood	itch	unting

READ & RESPOND: Activities based on Each Peach Pear Plum

I spy Plum Pie

● Find these items in *Each Peach Pear Plum*. Tick them off as you locate them.

☐ arrow	☐ duckling	☐ knife	
☐ basket	☐ dummy	☐ ladder	
☐ bow	☐ feather duster	☐ logs	
☐ broomstick	☐ fire poker	☐ peach	
☐ bucket	☐ flowerpot	☐ pear	
☐ butterfly	☐ frog	☐ pie	
☐ candle	☐ gun	☐ plum	
☐ cat	☐ horn	☐ rabbit	
☐ clock	☐ horse	☐ rolling pin	
☐ cup and saucer	☐ horseshoe	☐ sheep	
☐ cushion	☐ jug	☐ shepherd's crook	
☐ dripping tap	☐ kettle	☐ washing mangle	

Talk about it

Picture talk

Objective: To listen to others in class, ask relevant questions and follow instructions.
What you need: Copies of *Each Peach Pear Plum* and photocopiable page 22.
Cross-curricular link: Art.

What to do
● Organise the children to work in groups of four or five. Hand out photocopiable page 22 to each group. Ask the children to cut out the six question cards from the sheet and to place them face down on the table.
● Invite the children to open *Each Peach Pear Plum* at a random page and then to turn over three of the question cards. Tell them to discuss each question in relation to the illustration.
● Remind the children to listen to everyone's opinion and agree on group answers to the three questions.

● When the children are happy with their answers, ask them to turn to another random illustration and use it to discuss the remaining three questions.
● Two of the questions ask the children to think about what happened before and after the illustration. Encourage the children to think as widely as they like about these questions; explain that they do not need to follow the story. They might like to consider what happened to make Cinderella go up the stairs, or what led the Three Bears to go past Robin's den.

Differentiation
For older/more confident learners: Ask the children further questions about the illustrations, for example: *What is Robin Hood reading?*
For younger/less confident learners: Focus the children on discussing one or two of the questions from the photocopiable sheet.

Hide and seek

Objective: To engage with books through exploring and enacting interpretations.
What you need: Copies of *Each Peach Pear Plum*, cameras, props such as boxes, chairs, bookcases and curtains.
Cross-curricular link: ICT.

What to do
● Explain to the children that they are going to set up 'I spy' photographs.
● Organise the children to work in groups of four or five. Tell them to choose a place in the school for one or two of the group members to hide (for example, behind bookcases, under curtains or in boxes).
● Remind them that in *Each Peach Pear Plum* the person that is spied is visible in the picture, even if not obviously. Let them consider how they might achieve this. Could the children be camouflaged rather than hidden? Might they

just be peeping out of a big box?
● Give each group a camera and invite them to photograph the children hiding.
● If there is time available, ask them to choose a new hiding place for a different child.
● Print off the photographs and ask the groups to write simple 'I spy' captions. For example, 'I spy Chen and Emily'.
● Display the photos and captions in the class. What clues can they give to help spot the hider?
● As a class, work through the photographs playing 'I Spy'.

Differentiation
For older/more confident learners: Encourage the children to compose a two-line caption clue for their hiding place. For example, 'I spy Chen. He's behind something with books on it.'
For younger/less confident learners: Provide the children with sentence starters and a word bank to help them compose a short caption.

Talk about it

Traditional tale

> **Objective:** To present part of traditional stories, their own stories or work drawn from different parts of the curriculum for members of their own class.
> **What you need:** Copies of *Each Peach Pear Plum*.

What to do
● Organise the children into small groups and ask them to choose the original story of one of the characters from *Each Peach Pear Plum*. 'Cinderella' or 'Goldilocks and the Three Bears' would be the most straightforward. They could choose any fairy tale containing a Wicked Witch (such as 'Hansel and Gretel'). If the children select Robin Hood, allow them to focus on an event they remember. ('Tom Thumb' might be too challenging to work with.)
● Help each group to choose a suitable story

and then invite them to recall it in their group. Tell them to create an oral retelling of their story, taking turns to tell a part each.
● If the stories become too long, encourage them to focus on just the opening or a couple of key moments.
● Allow the children to tell their story, or part of their story, to the class. Can the rest of the class identify any parts that are missing or told in the wrong order?

> **Differentiation**
> **For older/more confident learners:** Challenge the children to tell the whole of their chosen story, ensuring that it is short and polished.
> **For younger/less confident learners:** Allow the children to work in pairs to tell the opening of their chosen story.

Would like to meet

> **Objective:** To identify the main events and characters in stories, and find specific information in simple texts.
> **What you need:** Copies of *Each Peach Pear Plum* and photocopiable page 23.
> **Cross-curricular link:** PSHE.

What to do
● Arrange the children into groups of three or four and tell them to imagine that they have been magically transported to 'Plum Land'.
● Provide each group with photocopiable page 23. Ask them to choose three characters from *Each Peach Pear Plum* whom they would most like to spend the day with (the left-hand column) and cut these out.
● Tell the groups to agree an order of preference for the three characters. Remind them to listen to each other's arguments.
● Extend their thinking about the characters,

for instance, they might love Cinderella but will they have to spend the day dusting? Alternatively, they might find it more fun to go flying with the Wicked Witch.
● Next, ask them to choose three characters from other fairy tales (either from the right-hand column or characters of their own choosing). Can they slot them into their ranking of the first three characters? Do they rank higher, lower or mixed in between?
● Discuss the groups' thoughts and enjoy the characters they have thrown into the mix.

> **Differentiation**
> **For older/more confident learners:** Challenge the children to discuss all of the characters from each column on the photocopiable sheet.
> **For younger/less confident learners:** Ask the children to have a meaningful discussion about just three of the characters from the sheet.

Talk about it

Cut-up nursery rhymes

Objective: To use syntax and context when reading for meaning.
What you need: Copies of *Each Peach Pear Plum*, photocopiable page 24.

What to do

● Ask the children to recall the nursery rhymes that are linked to *Each Peach Pear Plum*: 'Bye, Baby Bunting', 'Little Bo-Peep' and 'Jack and Jill'.
● Rehearse the nursery rhymes a couple of times (see pages 4 to 6).
● Arrange the children into small groups and hand out photocopiable page 24. Explain that the sheet has the three nursery rhymes on it, but they are all jumbled up. Can they sort them out?
● Tell the children to cut up the lines and then to discuss a strategy for sorting out the rhymes. Should they start with the first line of one rhyme and work through finding the lines in order? Or perhaps they could start with dividing the lines up into three piles, one for each rhyme?
● Ask: *What else will help you to get the lines in the right order?* (Plot and rhyme.)
● As a class, agree the order for each rhyme and encourage the children to join you in a recitation of each one.

Differentiation
For older/more confident learners: Remove a line from each nursery rhyme and invite the children to work out the missing line for each one.
For younger/less confident learners: Provide the children with the rhymes sorted into the three piles, ready to be rebuilt by them.

Everyone

Objective: To identify the main events and characters in stories, and find specific information in simple texts.
What you need: Copies of *Each Peach Pear Plum*, set of blank cards and whiteboard.

What to do

● Ask the children to open up their copies of *Each Peach Pear Plum* to the page showing the text *...EVERYONE!*
● With the children's help, name all the characters sitting round the Plum Pie. Write each name on a separate card or on a list on the interactive whiteboard.
● Together, use the illustration to reconstruct the story. Can the children remember which character appeared first? Who was next? How far through the book can the children remember? Are any of the characters difficult to recall?
● As you do this with the class, order the cards, or drag and drop the names on your list into order, until you have a list of the characters in order of appearance.
● Can the children remember who appeared together as the book unfolded? Were the Three Bears and Tom Thumb in the same picture at the beginning of the book? (No.)
● Establish how the pairing works and recall the book as a whole.

Differentiation
For older/more confident learners: Select a character and challenge the children to remember who came before and after them in the book.
For younger/less confident learners: Name a character and ask the children to flick through the book and locate the character's first appearance.

Picture talk

- Cut out the six question cards and place them face down.
- Choose a page from *Each Peach Pear Plum* and turn over three question cards. In your group, discuss your answers.

Look at this picture. Who is in this picture?	**Look at the characters in this picture.** What are they like?
Look at where this picture is set. What sort of place are we looking at?	**Look at what's happening in this picture.** What might have happened before?
Look at the characters in this picture. What are they doing?	**Look at what's happening in this picture.** What could happen next?

READ & RESPOND: Activities based on *Each Peach Pear Plum*

Would like to meet

● Choose three characters to meet from *Each Peach Pear Plum*. Cut them out and put them in order of preference.

● Pick three characters from other fairy tales and add these to the list. (Add your own character choices in the spaces, if you wish.)

Three Bears	Sleeping Beauty
Robin Hood	Hansel and Gretel
Cinderella	Seven Dwarves
Tom Thumb	
Wicked Witch	

SECTION 5

Cut-up nursery rhymes

● These three nursery rhymes are mixed up. Cut out the cards and put them together again.

Little Bo-Peep has lost her sheep
To fetch a pail of water.
Daddy's gone a-hunting,
Bye, Baby Bunting,
To wrap the Baby Bunting in.
And doesn't know where to find them;
Jack and Jill went up the hill
And Jill came tumbling after.
Gone to get a rabbit skin
Wagging their tails behind them.
Jack fell down and broke his crown
Leave them alone, and they'll come home,

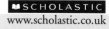
www.scholastic.co.uk

READ & RESPOND: Activities based on Each Peach Pear Plum

Get writing

Guide to Plum Land

> **Objective:** To maintain consistency in non-narrative, including purpose and tense.
> **What you need:** Copies of *Each Peach Pear Plum*, leaflets about local attractions.
> **Cross-curricular link:** Geography.

What to do
● With the class, share leaflets of local attractions and discuss their features, such as maps, advice, information, and so on.
● Tell the children that, together, they will be creating a visitor leaflet for 'Plum Land'.
● Gather a list of suggestions as to what might be on the leaflet and from this agree a list of sections to include. For example:
  ● Visiting Plum Land
  ● Walks in the area
  ● Who you may see
  ● Places you could visit
  ● Map
  ● Advice to travellers (such as 'Watch out for bears with guns')
● Invite small groups or pairs of children to create one of the sections for the leaflet.
● When the children have finished, fold a poster-sized sheet of paper into three landscape columns to make a leaflet and stick on the various sections created by the children.

> **Differentiation**
> **For older/more confident learners:** Challenge the children to create the walks section and general introduction.
> **For younger/less confident learners:** Encourage the children to create a simple 'Who you might see' section starting 'Look out for…'.

Plum Land story

> **Objective:** To create short simple texts on paper and on screen that combine words with images (and sounds).
> **What you need:** Copies of *Each Peach Pear Plum*, paper and photocopiable page 28.
> **Cross-curricular link:** Geography.

What to do
● Hand out photocopiable page 28 and explain that this will be the setting for the children's own story.
● Ask: *Who's in your story and what happens?* Perhaps someone or something is lost and someone is searching for them or it.
● Tell the children to make notes in the boxes about what might happen in each location. Can they think of a paired problem and solution, or a solution and new problem for each? Encourage the children to end on a solution.
● Next, invite the children to create an eight-page booklet by folding a piece of paper accordingly.
● Ask the children to write the title of their story on the front cover and then start writing their story on the first left-hand page, illustrating it on the right. Encourage them to pattern their story with problems followed by solutions and to link some of the areas in their story.
● Encourage volunteers to read and display their stories in class.

> **Differentiation**
> **For older/more confident learners:** Challenge the children to use four, five or more locations in their story.
> **For younger/less confident learners:** Ask the children to focus on a story scenario using just two locations, so the story starts in one place and moves to the second location by the end.

Get writing

Character rhymes

> **Objective:** To make adventurous word and language choices appropriate to the style and purpose of the text.
> **What you need:** Copies of *Each Peach Pear Plum*.
> **Cross-curricular link:** Music.

What to do

● Write one paired line from the rhyme on the board or return to one of the extracts (pages 8 to 10). Ask for a volunteer to circle the rhyming words. Talk about the metre of the rhyme by counting the beats in each line.

● Explain to the children that they are going to work in groups to create pairs of rhyming lines for characters of their choice. Challenge them to move away from the 'I spy…' opening and move towards a line such as:

'I was going for a walk,
And I saw Jack up his beanstalk.'

● Organise the children into small groups to create a rhyming pair. Encourage them to first agree on a character and then to discuss rhyming words. When they have found two words that rhyme, encourage them to make their couplet with them. If they cannot think of a rhyme for their character's name, invite them to try something that is associated with that character, such as Humpty Dumpty's wall.

● When everyone has finished, try putting the rhyming couplets together into one long poem and display it in the classroom.

> **Differentiation**
> **For older/more confident learners:** Invite the children to make two linked rhyming couplets.
> **For younger/less confident learners:** Encourage the children to find words that rhyme with their favourite character and provide lines for them to complete.

Each Dog Frog Sheep

> **Objective:** To use key features of narrative in their own writing.
> **What you need:** Copies of *Each Peach Pear Plum*, photocopiable page 29.

What to do

● Look together at the animals that appear throughout the book; they often reappear from page to page.

● Point out the mini stories about these animals: the rabbits are concerned about the hunting bears, the dog eats and sleeps, the bluebirds move from well to bush and then narrowly miss an arrow.

● Ask the children to think of things the animals could say. For example, the frog could say 'He's sleeping so peacefully' or 'Oh dear, he's in trouble!'.

● Hand out photocopiable page 29 and ask the children to write a suggestion for what each animal might say at a certain point in the story where they appear.

● Invite the children to choose one of the animals and draft a short diary entry for that animal to include where they went, what they did and who they saw.

> **Differentiation**
> **For older/more confident learners:** Challenge the children to imagine that their animal meets one of the other animals in the story and to include their conversation in the diary entry.
> **For younger/less confident learners:** Ask the children to write a speech bubble for just two of the animals from the book.

Get writing

Characters for writing

> **Objective:** To draw on knowledge and experience of texts in deciding and planning what and how to write.
> **What you need:** Copies of *Each Peach Pear Plum*, card and photocopiable page 30.
> **Cross-curricular link:** PSHE.

What to do

● Create two sets of character cards with the following names on them. **Pile A:** Cinderella, Robin Hood, Wicked Witch, Three Bears, Tom Thumb. **Pile B:** Goldilocks, Three Little Pigs, Puss in Boots, Big Bad Wolf, Fairy Godmother.
● Allow the children to take turns to pick a card from each of the piles, giving them, for example, Cinderella and Three Little Pigs.
● Invite them to imagine that their two characters meet in the woods, in the setting for *Each Peach Pear Plum* or in another setting. Ask: *Are they friends or are they afraid of each other? What do they do when they meet: dance, fight or perhaps go on an adventure?*

● Hand out photocopiable page 30 and ask the children to fill in the boxes for their chosen characters. Encourage them to think carefully about what each character is like and what they might say.
● Once the children have created their characters, invite them to plan a simple story involving the two characters, where they go and what they do, with a beginning, middle and end.
● Allow time for the children to tell their story a couple of times to a talk partner and then to write it down.

> **Differentiation**
> **For older/more confident learners:** Encourage the children to work on a story plan involving three characters – picking two characters from one of the piles.
> **For younger/less confident learners:** Allow the children to focus on completing the sheet without planning a story.

Postcard

> **Objective:** To draw on knowledge and experience of texts in deciding and planning what and how to write.
> **What you need:** Copies of *Each Peach Pear Plum*, holiday postcards and individual postcard-sized cards.

What to do

● With the class, look at some holiday postcards and agree on the consistent features: picture, short note, address and stamp.
● Hand out the blank postcards and ask the children to select a character in *Each Peach Pear Plum* to be the author of their postcard. Encourage them to think carefully about who they are going to send it to. (Perhaps Cinderella will write to one of the ugly sisters or to Sleeping Beauty.)

● Remind them of the features they should include and give them time to complete the different elements.
● Ensure the children have copies of the book for stimulus, but explain that they can either write directly about the character's experiences in the story, or about something that might have happened later.

> **Differentiation**
> **For older/more confident learners:** Challenge the children to write a reply from the new character, or the next postcard sent from the same character after a disaster has struck.
> **For younger/less confident learners:** Support the children to write a couple of simple sentences in character about what happens to them in the book.

Plum Land story

- Examine this picture and write what happens in your story at each of the five locations.

Illustration © 1978, Janet and Allan Ahlberg.

READ & RESPOND: Activities based on Each Peach Pear Plum

Each Dog Frog Sheep

● Find these animals in *Each Peach Pear Plum*. What might they be saying? (You can choose which point in the story to use.)

Illustrations © 2012, Mike Phillips (Beehive Illustration).

Characters for writing

- Complete the grid for two characters who are going to meet in your story.

	Character 1	Character 2
Character name		
What are they like?		
What could they say in a story?		
Where would they go?		
How do they meet the other character?		
What would they do?		
What would happen in the end?		

Assessment

Assessment advice

At a first reading, *Each Peach Pear Plum* can seem almost like a nonsense nursery rhyme. However, when looked at in conjunction with the images, many narrative strands can be found to talk about plot, character and setting.

Good assessment for learning involves children identifying their own progress. When assessing the children's understanding of the work they have been doing on *Each Peach Pear Plum*, we need to assess if the children have moved forwards in their understanding of:
● Narrative order: Are the children able to recall narrative order?
● Plot: Can they talk about how one thing leads to another?
● Setting: Do the children see how setting and journey locations contribute to the story?

Look together at one of the pages from *Each Peach Pear Plum*. Can the children talk about what will be on the next double-page? For example, if you show them the picture of Mother Hubbard in the cellar, can they talk about who

will be on the next page and what she will be doing? (Cinderella will be dusting.) Can they make the connection between what they know about the character and what they do in the book? Can they remember who is 'spied' on that page? (Three Bears.) Turn the page to confirm. How far through the book can they go?

Use this as the basis to ask the children to think about three main characters, what they did and where they did it. Identify these three questions and encourage the children to assess one another on their identification of these story features. To extend the assessment, invite the children to identify the same story features in other stories featuring these well-known characters.

Photocopiable page 32 can be used to assess the children's understanding of the connections made in the story. Work with the children individually to assess their understanding of the links between the characters and the events in the book.

Making connections

> **Objective:** To visualise and comment on events, characters and ideas.
> **What you need:** Copies of *Each Peach Pear Plum*, photocopiable page 32 and writing materials.

What to do
● Prior to the start of the lesson, cut out the four pictures from photocopiable page 32 and place them face down on a table.
● Explain to the children that *Each Peach Pear Plum* contains many connections and that they need to identify some of them.

● Invite each child to turn over two of the pictures and to explain the connection between the two events (they may find more than one).
● In the end all the characters do meet at the picnic, but can the child discuss any other ways in which the characters are connected? Some combinations will be easier than others. For instance, the children may devise simple links, such as 'Bo-Peep is on the same hill as the Wicked Witch'.
● Can they suggest more complex links, such as 'the Three Bears send the Baby floating past Bo-Peep'?

Making connections

● Cut out the four pictures and place them face down. Choose two and say how the characters meet or are connected.

Illustrations © 1978, Janet and Allan Ahlberg.

READ & RESPOND: Activities based on Each Peach Pear Plum